Why is light given to those in misery, and life to the bitter in soul, to those who long for death that does not come, who search for it more than for hidden treasure, who are filled with gladness and rejoice when they reach the grave?... I have no peace, no quietness; I have no rest, but only turmoil.
- Job 3:20-22,26 (NIV)

I0117032

Why Is Life So Difficult?

Reflections and Suggestions

Max Malikow

Why Is Life So Difficult?

Copyright © 2019 by Max Malikow

Library of Congress Control Number: 2019933744

ISBN 9781732437968

Unless otherwise noted Scripture is taken from the New International Version (NIV) of the Holy Bible.

Dedications

To Meredith Rayna Goodman: Carl Sandberg writes, "Never will a time come when the most marvelous recent invention is as marvelous as a newborn baby."

To Diane Malikow: Who makes life more pleasant for all who encounter her.

To Dr. James A. Manganello: To whom I am indebted and who I appreciate more with each passing year.

To Terry Riley: Who has enriched my life by being my friend.

Acknowledgments

On September 17, 2018, while this book was being written, Professor Daniel N. Robinson passed away at age 81. If the love of family and friends, admiration of colleagues, and scholarly contributions constitute a good life then, indeed, his was a good life. His encyclopedic knowledge of both psychology and philosophy was beyond impressive, it was awe-inspiring. On several occasions I have said to my own students, "When I grow up, I want to be like Daniel Robinson." This goal, however laudable, will never be attained - it is beyond my capability. His imprint on this book came through his brilliant lectures and writing. It is fitting to acknowledge his part in this writing project.

Preface

Life is difficult. This is a great truth, one of the greatest truths.
                                                    - M. Scott Peck

Over the 33 years in which I have practiced psychotherapy many patients and clients, in various ways, have asked, "Why is life so difficult?" Well, one thing that makes life difficult for any therapist is trying to answer this question in a relevant, encouraging way. Viktor Frankl, a psychiatrist and Holocaust survivor, unflinchingly takes on this question in the epilogue of his classic, *Man's Search for Meaning*. There he speaks of tragic optimism, his belief that life's three unavoidable tragedies (pain, guilt, and death) can be optimized. In another classic, *The Road Less Travelled*, another psychiatrist, M. Scott Peck, writes, "Once we truly know that life is difficult - once we truly understand and accept it - then life is no longer difficult. Because once it is accepted, the fact that life is difficult no longer matters" (1978, p. 15).

I agree with Frankl and Peck that a considerable part of everyone's life consists of solving problems. While some problems can and should be avoided, many others should be confronted, lest life be made more difficult by avoiding them. The pages that follow address four questions:

1. What is a difficult life?

2. Why shouldn't life be difficult?

3. How is life made more difficult than it has to be?

4. Is a good life possible?

In the spirit of Frankl and Peck I address these questions redemptively. Merely agreeing with people that life is difficult is insufficient to help them.

There is a sequence to this book. Each chapter provides a response to its respective question culminating in the encouraging conclusion that a good life is possible in spite of the reality of challenges, disappointments, and even suffering.

Max Malikow
Syracuse, New York
December 24, 2018

Table of Contents

Introduction

*My mother groaned, my father wept, into the dangerous world
I leapt.*
                                    - William Blake, "Infant Sorrow"

In *A farewell to Arms* Ernest Hemingway provides an
eloquent characterization of the difficulty of life:

> If people bring so much courage to this world the
> world has to kill them to break them, so of course it
> kills them. The world breaks every one and afterward
> many are strong at the broken places. Those that it
> does not break, it kills. It kills the very good and the
> very gentle and the very brave impartially. If you are
> none of these you can be sure it will kill you too but
> there will be no special hurry (2014, p. 317).

In the introduction to *The Human Predicament* the
evolution of that book's title is explained:

> It is not unusual for the title of a book to change as the
> writing project progresses. One of several working
> titles for this book was *The Human Situation* until it
> became apparent that "situation" is a neutral word and,
> therefore, inadequately descriptive. "Situation" was
> replaced by "predicament" owing to the latter's more
> precise description of a status that is not merely a

circumstance, but one that is difficult, troubling, and, perhaps, perplexing (Malikow, 2013, p.1).

Both of these quotations assert life is difficult, which is to say meeting responsibilities, pursuing pleasure, and avoiding pain are not easily accomplished. Siddhartha Gautama, the founder of Buddhism, characterized life as suffering in the first of the Four Noble Truths. Jesus told his disciples, "In this world you will have tribulation" (John 16:33, NIV). Psychiatrist and Holocaust survivor Viktor Frankl taught that pain is one of life's three unavoidable tragedies. (Guilt and death are the other two.) And, in *Pet Cemetery*, Stephen King writes, "Life sucks, and then you die" (2018). These communications from diverse sources agree: life is difficult for everyone.

Notwithstanding, this book is not intended for everyone. Obviously it was not written for those rare individuals who do not believe life is difficult. Although unsupported historically, Marie Antoinette, wife of Louis XVI, is notorious for having said, "Let them eat cake" when told the peasants had no bread. This book would be of no interest to anyone who is nescient of the suffering of others. Neither is this book written for anyone who is living a difficult life but unaware of doing so. A literary example is Lenny, a character in the classic novel *Of Mice and Men*, an intellectually disabled man who is naive to the harshness of life, including his own. This book is intended for those who are living a difficult life, perhaps to the point of despair, and curious about why life is so difficult and what can be done about it. This is the audience Frankl had in mind when he wrote *Man's Search for Meaning*. In the introduction he explains,

> I wanted simply to convey to the reader by way of a concrete example that life holds a potential meaning under any conditions, even the most miserable ones. And I thought if that point were demonstrated in a situation as extreme as that in a concentration camp, my book might gain a hearing. I therefore felt responsible for writing down what I had gone through, for I thought it might be helpful to people who are prone to despair (1959, p. 16).

Like Frankl, I hope to encourage readers to persevere through a difficult life by considering what they expect from life and from where their expectations came. In addition, I address various ways in which many people make life more difficult than it has to be. Finally, given that life is difficult, I respond to the question, "Is a good life possible?"

Merely admitting that life is difficult and bemoaning that reality provides neither comfort nor encouragement while passing through this vale of tears. However, even an unfortunate life can be analyzed by the one living it in such a way that the intolerable becomes tolerable if not satisfying. Baseball legend Lou Gehrig epitomized reflection and reframing when he assessed his life while dying from amyotrophic lateral sclerosis, a neurodegenerative disease in which the body's muscles continually deteriorate. In his famous speech given at Yankee Stadium on "Lou Gehrig Appreciation Day" on July 4, 1939 he spoke these words to an audience of 62,000 fans:

> Fans, for the past two weeks you have been reading about the bad break I got. Yet today I consider myself the luckiest man on the face of this earth. ...When you have a father and a mother who work all their lives so you can have an education and build your body - it's a blessing. When you have a wife who has been a tower of strength and shown more courage than you dreamed existed - that's the finest I know. So I close in saying that I may have had a tough break, but I have an awful lot to live for (2008).

I. What is a difficult Life?

May the day of my birth perish ... May those who curse days curse that day.

- Job 3:3,8 (NIV)

In a letter to a fellow writer the English poet Alexander Pope writes: "I have many years ago magnified in my own mind and repeated to you, a ninth Beatitude, added to the eight in Scripture: Blessed is the man who expects nothing, for he shall not be disappointed" (2000, p. 117). Even if the letter's recipient, John Gay, did not object to Pope's amendment to the Beatitudes, another writer did take exception. G.K. Chesterton countered Pope's proposal with these words:

> The man who said, "Blessed is he that expecteth nothing, for he shall not be disappointed," put the eulogy quite inadequately and even falsely. The truth (is) "Blessed is he that expecteth nothing, for he shall be gloriously surprised." The man who expects nothing sees redder roses than common men can see, and greener grass, and a more startling sun (2001, p. 24).

Pope's ninth Beatitude is impossible to actualize. No one could live a life devoid of expectation. Moreover, even in theory, it would not be effective because the non-expecting man would be conscious of his strategy. He would know he

Max Malikow

eschews expectation because he fears the disappointment of unfulfilled desire. Such a man would be akin to someone who does not answer the phone in order to avoid hearing the bad news he knows awaits him. Chesterton's position is the more tenable. If a man could get himself to expect nothing he would be pleasantly surprised by the most ordinary of things. His liberation from expecting anything would enable him to enjoy the commonplace pleasures unnoticed by most people. An acquaintance at a party where you didn't expect to know anyone is appreciated all the more because of non-expectation.

What does it mean to say life is difficult? It means avoiding pain and pursuing pleasure require considerable effort and that many of life's activities are devoted to reaching and maintaining a state of physical and emotional ease. A characteristic of addicts is their determination to live a pain-free, pleasure-full life. The desirability of such a life is understandable but an impossibility as well as imprudent. In real life there are times when discomfort contributes to eventual life enrichment. People who resist discussing or doing something by saying, "I'm not comfortable with that," fail to realize comfort matters only when buying a mattress. Additionally, the unbridled pursuit of pleasure never results in the joyful life it advertises. The writer of Ecclesiastes states, "I denied myself nothing my eyes desired; I refused my heart no pleasure" (2:10, NIV). Still, he concludes, "everything was meaningless, a chasing after the wind; nothing was gained under the sun (2:11, NIV). One of life's difficulties and disappointments is pain-avoidance and pleasure-pursuit, two paths that seem to lead to an easy life, often turn out to be dead ends.

Another characteristic of addicts is their irresponsibility. The world of an addict is ever diminishing; all interests and activities that do not support the addiction evaporate. Ultimately, all responsibilities are jettisoned until the only remaining entities are the addict and the addiction. But a person does not have to be an addict to be irresponsible. Desmond Hatchett is not an addict, but his irresponsibility is undeniable:

> Desmond Hatchett, 33, is something of a local legend in Knoxville, Tennessee. In 2009, in a t.v. interview, he proclaimed, "I'm done!" - that he wouldn't father any more children. Now, with 30 children by 11 women, he wants a break on child-support payments. The youngest is a toddler; the oldest is 14. Hatchett has a minimum wage job, and he struggles to make ends meet. He's required to turn over 50 percent of his wages for child support - the maximum under law (*The Huffington Post*, 05/18/2012).

Hatchett's freedom created paternal responsibilities he is not meeting and doesn't seem to want to meet. Sigmund Freud believed, "Most people do not really want freedom, because freedom involves responsibility, and most people are frightened of responsibility" (Egan, 2016, p. 205). Frankl expresses the same thought in *Man's Search for Meaning*:

"(F)reedom is in danger of degenerating into mere arbitrariness unless it is lived in terms of responsibleness. *That is why I recommend that the Statue of Liberty on the East Coast be supplemented by a Statue of Responsibility on the West Coast* (1959, p. 156). Responsible people meet obligations and are answerable for their conduct. As Frankl observed, freedom must be understood in terms of its accompanying responsibility. And, for many people, this is a frightening reality, as Freud asserted. Stress, the perceived inability to cope with a situation, is often created by responsibility and explains, in part, why life is difficult.

Another source of stress is the question of life's meaning. The renowned psychiatrist Irvin Yalom maintains the meaning of life is one of four philosophical issues present in psychotherapy:

> I have found that four givens are particularly relevant to psychotherapy: the inevitability of death for each of us and for those we love; the freedom to make our lives as we will; our ultimate aloneness; and, finally, the absence of any obvious meaning or sense to life (1989, pp. 4-5).

Yalom is not referring to the meaning of humankind's existence but to each individual's concern with the meaning and purpose of her life. An apocryphal quotation attributed to Mark Twain expressing the same concern is, "The two most important days of your life are the day you were born and the

8

day you find out why." Carl Jung, Freud's contemporary and erstwhile collaborator, addresses the significance of *existential angst*, the phenomenon in which a person is confronted with his finite existence and forced to come to terms with it. In *Modern Man in Search of a Soul* he writes,

> Among my patients from many countries, all of them educated persons, there is a considerable number who came to see me, not because they were suffering from a neurosis, but because they could find no meaning in life ... (1933, p. 231).

The manifestation of this confrontation may vary from person to person, but nearly everyone gives thought to whether her life has significance.

Closely related to stress is anxiety - a feeling of worry, nervousness, or unease about an imminent event or something with an uncertain outcome. It is so common the Danish philosopher Soren Kierkegaard considered anxiety the natural state of human beings:

> Just as a physician might say that there very likely is not one single living human being who is completely healthy, so anyone who really knows mankind might say that there is not one single living human being who does not despair a little, who does not secretly harbor an unrest, an inner strife, a disharmony, an anxiety about an unknown something or a something he does

not even dare try to know, an anxiety about some possibility in existence or an anxiety about himself, so that, just as the physician speaks of going around with an illness in the body, he walks around with a sickness, carries around a sickness of the spirit that signals its presence at rare intervals in and through an anxiety he cannot explain (1980, p. 22).

William James, celebrated as a philosopher and psychologist, posited four unknowables concerning human existence. He believed it cannot be known with certainty,

- whether God exists
- whether free will is a reality
- whether there is an afterlife
- whether there is such a thing as moral obligation

For centuries philosophers and theologians have made arguments for and against each of these unknowables. But to argue for or against the validity of something is not to irrefutably establish it as a fact. To be uncertain about God, free will, immortality, and moral obligations generates universal anxiety. It's no wonder Kierkegaard considered anxiety the natural state of human beings.

According to a study conducted by Harvard psychology professor Gordon Allport there are 17,953 personality traits (1936). If centuries of philosophical, theological, and psychological reflection and writing can be trusted then self-discipline is at or near the top of the list of desirable traits. Self-discipline is the ability to do what ought to be done when it ought to be done in spite of resistant feelings. When neuroscientist Robert Sapolsky was asked to define the brain's frontal cortex - the place where deliberation occurs - he defined it as the part of the brain that "is responsible for getting you to do the harder thing when the harder thing is the better/right thing to do" (2018). There is no weakness for which self-discipline cannot compensate and there's no strength that will matter if self-discipline is lacking. The all-time bestselling self-help psychology book consists entirely of extolling it (Peck, 1978); it is one of the five components of *emotional intelligence* (Goleman, 1995); and one of the *Four Cardinal Virtues.*

The necessity of self-discipline for life contentment also explains, in part, why life is difficult. Self-discipline is not innate; like a muscle, it is developed by exercise. Shakespeare understood this and wrote, "Assume a virtue if you have it not" (*Hamlet*, 3.4). Aristotle believed many of life's failures, including moral failures, result from negligence in developing good habits. Will Durant, in his classic, *The Story of Philosophy*, expresses his agreement with Aristotle: "we do not act rightly because we have virtue or excellence, but we rather have these because we have acted rightly ... we are what we repeatedly do. Excellence, then, is not an act but a habit (1926, p. 76).

Unmet expectations, pursuit of pleasure, avoidance of pain, responsibility owing to freedom, life's meaning, anxiety from uncertainty and unknowables, and mastery of self-discipline combine to make life difficult. In her 2008 commencement address at Harvard, 41-year-old J.K. Rowling, the first billionaire author, shared this thought concerning life's difficulty:

> Given a time machine or a Time Turner, I would tell my 21-year-old self that personal happiness lies in knowing that life is not a check-list of acquisition or achievement. Your qualifications, your CV, are not your life, though you will meet many people of my age and older who confuse the two. Life is difficult, and complicated, and beyond anyone's total control, and the humility to know that will enable you to survive its vicissitudes (Smith, 2008).

II. Why Shouldn't Life Be Difficult?

There is really nothing more to say - except why. But since why is difficult to handle, one must take refuge in how.
                                                    - Toni Morrison

The literary scholar C.S. Lewis recounted an experience from his childhood when he left home to attend boarding school. He was met at the train station by a man who gave him a ride to the school. En route Lewis attempted to engage in conversation with the driver by commenting that he didn't expect the town they were passing through to look as it did. The driver, who was the school's headmaster, asked Lewis if he had ever seen the town before. When Lewis said he had not, the man then asked him why he had any expectation of what the town would look like. Lewis admitted he had no reason to expect the town to look any particular way and realized even casual observations would be challenged in the next phase of his education.

Like that town, life is what it is apart from any expectation that it should be otherwise. Why should anyone assume that life should *not* be difficult? The existential philosopher and novelist Albert Camus employed the term *absurdity* when referring an individual's unwarranted expectations of meaning, satisfaction, and happiness in life. Camus begins his celebrated essay, "The Myth of Sisyphus," with a description of the eternal fate of Sisyphus, the King of Ephyra, who antagonized the gods with his passion for life and hatred of death.

> The gods had condemned Sisyphus to ceaselessly rolling a rock to the top of a mountain, whence the stone would fall back of its own weight. They had thought with some reason that there is no more dreadful punishment than futile and hopeless labor (1955, p. 88).

Another existentialist, Simone de Beauvoir, agreed with the gods and writes:

> There is no more obnoxious way to punish a man than to force him to perform acts which make no sense to him, as when one empties and fills the same ditch indefinitely, when one makes soldiers who are being punished march up and down, when one forces a schoolboy to copy lines (2014).

Camus used Sisyphus as a metaphor for the repetitive tasks that constitute a workingman's life. In this vein he writes:

> If this myth is tragic, that is because its hero is conscious. Where would his torture be, indeed, if at every step the hope of succeeding upheld him. The workingman of today works everyday in his life at the same tasks, and this fate is no less absurd. But it is

tragic only at the rare moments when it becomes conscious (1955, pp. 88-90).

A contemporary philosopher, Thomas Nagel, also addresses the absurdity of life. He believes, "(We) vacillate between two different perspectives on our own activities. When we are involved in doing something, we normally think we are doing something worthwhile" (Wartenberg, 2008, p. 120). However, Nagel adds that a second perspective might invade our thinking and belittle our labor:

> If I'm a violinist, I have to think there's something significant about playing the violin or I won't be able to engage in the strenuous practice required to become skilled. ... If I think about the fact that I am just one human being on a planet in one solar system in a vast galaxy that is but a small part of an unimaginably huge universe, my own violin playing just won't seem something that makes a difference at all (p. 120).

Surprisingly, Camus concludes, "One must imagine Sisyphus as happy" (1955, p. 91). Why? Because he recognizes the absurdity of life and is fully aware it is futile "to demand reasonableness of a universe that does not, that cannot provide it" (Wartenberg, p. 115). Sisyphus labors at the work from which he cannot escape without the delusion that a blissful life awaits him at a future time in another place. Unlike those who yearn for heaven, Sisyphus knows, "Life is a long preparation for something that never happens" (Yeats, 2014).

Is there any sentient entity that has an easy life? Nature itself sends the clarion message that life is difficult. Frogs eat flies, making life difficult for flies; snakes eat frogs, making life difficult for frogs; alligators eat snakes, making life difficult for snakes; and men kill alligators to make shoes and handbags, making life difficult for alligators. As for men, Thomas Hobbes assessed the life of man in the state of nature "as solitary, poor, nasty, brutish, and short" (1994, p. 76). There is no basis for the assumption that life should be easy. Further, how could anyone know what life *ought* to be like? Psychologist and author Wayne Dyer conducted an informal experiment when he interviewed married couples, asking them what they valued most from their years together. Most of them responded that they appreciated the early years when they struggled, often financially, and persevered. Dyer followed up by asking what they wanted most for their children. Almost all of them said, "We don't want our children to struggle the way we struggled." Ironically, they wanted their children deprived of the very experiences they valued most.

What if life were not difficult?

The antithesis of a difficult life would be an *easy* life. Although such a life is not a possibility the benefit of pondering this imaginary existence is the perspective it provides for confronting real life. An easy life would have no challenges making it a life without achievement. (Achievement is one of psychologist Henry Murray's 27 universal human needs [1938]). In addition, an easy life would be a life without fear or misfortune, making heroism an impossibility. Without overcoming fear and acting courageously or overcoming misfortune and showing resilience or persevering and accomplishing survival or some other admirable goal there can be no heroism. Lest heroism seem unimportant, consider the ubiquitous nature of heroic stories:

> Heroic stories are discoverable in every culture and every era. They provide compelling evidence that people believe, and have always believed, they can improve themselves and, thereby, make the world a better place even in the absence of a divine being or mythical superheroes (Malikow, 2017, p. 13).

Of course, if life were easy for everyone there would be no need for heroes. A life of continuous comfort would provide no need for heroic action and no incentive for any action that involves risking failure or disappointment. Would most people want a life of uninterrupted, unearned comfort? Such a life would approximate the stereotype of heaven as an eternity of lounging on a cloud or other soft surface listening to harp music. (This is something few, if any, of us would want for five minutes in this life, let alone for eternity.) A well-known thought experiment devised by Hilary Putnam, a philosopher and mathematician, suggests a life of unremitting pleasure is something most people would forgo. His "brain in a vat" hypothetical existence was intended to disprove the belief that everything seen or heard is untethered to reality.

If that were the case, Professor Putnam argued, then a human brain would be no different from a brain in a vat placed there by a mad scientist. Human brains, however, employ words based on the things they refer to, which requires some kind of contact with those things. So the brain in a vat - call him Oscar – could not formulate the sentence "I am a brain in a vat," because Oscar has no experience of a real brain or a real vat. Rather, he would actually be saying something like "I'm the image of a brain in the image of a vat" (Weber, 2016).

If Putnam's thought experiment is applied to the possibility of experiencing continuous comfort, how would most people respond to the opportunity to have their brains removed, placed in a vat, and stimulated to experience uninterrupted pleasure? Would they choose continuous, disembodied comfort over a real life punctuated by both pain and comfort? At least some people would reject this opportunity, thereby demonstrating a life of ease is not the ultimate life. (This hypothetical has been presented to dozens of my students over the years and nearly all of them said they would opt for the real life.)

William James defined happiness as "persistent enjoyment" and although he believed uninterrupted pleasure was unattainable, he suggests, for some people, it is the ultimate motivation for human activity:

> If we were to ask the question, "What is human life's chief concern?" one of the answers we should receive would be: "It is happiness." How to gain, how to keep, how to recover happiness is in fact for most men the secret motive for all they do, and of all they are willing to endure (1902, p. 77).

This belief has intellectual appeal since happiness is rarely, if ever, spoken of as something intermediate. Happiness is nearly always referred to as the destination rather than a prerequisite to something else. But if the hunt rather than the prize is what life is all about then the work of gaining, recovering, and striving to keep happiness is, in the final analysis, the best possible life.

Another possibility is the best possible life for nescient beings is not a life of striving for mere survival but a difficult life that strengthens them. Friedrich Nietzsche believed adversity can build character and wrote, "That which does not kill me makes me stronger" (Dargay, 2018). But stronger for what purpose? To develop endurance for more adversity? If this is the case then no one should be born. Philosopher David Benatar believes the only remedy for a difficult life, which everybody has, is for people to stop having children. He argues since no one has a choice concerning his existence everyone's birth constitutes a denial of free will, a fundamental human right. In addition, he asserts whatever pleasure might come from an individual's existence that life also will include pain. Since existence can be avoided altogether there is no need for anyone to experience any pain. Accordingly he writes,

> Although the good things in one's life make it go better than it otherwise would have gone, one could not have been deprived by their absence if one had not existed. Those who never exist cannot be deprived. However, by coming into existence one does suffer quite serious harms that could not have befallen one had one not come into existence" (2006, p. 1).

Benatar's approach to life (if it can be called an approach to life) has not gone unchallenged. In spite of pain being unavoidable, human reproduction continues to the present with no end in sight. Procreation owes itself to the innate evolutionary drive to perpetuate the species. Nature militates against *antinatalism*, the term for Benatar's philosophical position.

A man named Job is the biblical paradigm of suffering. After experiencing one calamity after another he beseeches God to explain the reason for these catastrophic events. Rather than an explanation, Job is told he is impudent to question God:

Then the Lord answered Job out of the storm. He said: Who is this that darkens my counsel with words without knowledge? Brace yourself like a man; I will question you, and you shall answer me. Where were you when I laid the earth's foundation? Tell me, if you understand? (Job 38: 1-4, NIV).

Job concedes he is not competent to question the Almighty and humbles himself: "I am unworthy - how can I reply to you? I put my hand over my mouth. I spoke once, but I have no answer - twice, but I will say no more" (40: 4-5, NIV). Alexander Pope described the impossibility of comprehending the larger picture that would make sense of suffering if that picture could be understood by mere mortals:

All nature is but art, unknown to thee;
All chance, direction, which thou canst not see;
All discord, harmony, not understood;
All partial evil, universal good:
And, spite of pride, in erring reason's spite,
One truth is clear, Whatever is, is right (2018).

Job is bewildered by the tragedies that have invaded his life because he has done nothing to deserve them. The simplistic belief that bad things happen only to bad people as punishment for their misdeeds does not apply to him. Like "Little Bill" Daggett, the sheriff in the Academy Award winning western, "The Unforgiven," Job believes his fate is undeserved. Before being killed by an outlaw named Will Munny, Daggett says, "I don't deserve this ... to die like this" (1992). Before firing the fatal shot Munny replies, "Deserve's got nothing to do with it" (1992).

III. How Is Life Made More Difficult Than It Has To Be?

This life's hard, but it's harder if you're stupid.
- George V. Higgins

In addition to maintaining the assumption that life should not be difficult there are numerous other ideas and behaviors that make life more difficult than it otherwise would be. Life is hard enough without them and there is no benefit derived from any of them. There are at least five ways by which life can be made more difficult than it has to be.

Cognitive Distortion

Aaron T. Beck, a psychiatrist and the founder of the therapeutic approach known as CBT (Cognitive Behavioral Therapy), believes much depression results from negative thoughts that are illogical and unsupportable. He coined the term "cognitive triad" for the unwarranted beliefs many depressed people have concerning themselves, the world, and the future. Drawing illogical conclusions and believing things that cannot stand up to scrutiny make life excessively arduous and exhausting. As Mark Twain put it (if he is the one who actually said it): "It ain't what you don't know that gets you into trouble. It's what you know for sure that just ain't so."

Beck does not posit all negative thoughts are groundless; only those that are baseless are challenged in CBT. Like Socrates, Beck believes an examined life is the best possible life. The main cognitive distortions according to Beck are:

- Arbitrary Inference: drawing conclusions from insufficient or no evidence
- Selective Attention: drawing conclusions on the basis of chosen parts of a situation
- Overgeneralization: making sweeping conclusions based on a single event
- Magnification: exaggerating the importance of an undesirable event
- Minimization: underplaying the significance of a positive event
- Personalization: attributing negative feelings of others to oneself

People who hold unsupportable beliefs about themselves, the world, and the future tend to over-trust their feelings. Consequently, they often draw a conclusion based on emotion as a starting point and then construct a rationale for the conclusion.

Moral Failures

There is a difference between being *rational* and *rationalizing*. The former means using logic and evidence to formulate explanations. The latter means attempting to justify oneself with explanations that are plausible but actually not true. According to Freud, rationalization is a defense mechanism unconsciously employed to keep from admitting to wrongdoing or an erroneous belief. "When people's actions differ from their morals, they begin to rationalize ... The bigger the dissonance, the larger the rationalization, and the longer it lasts, the less immoral it seems" (Nisen and Groth, 2012). Because it operates unconsciously, rationalization leads to self-deception. Self-deception, as with any departure from reality, makes life more difficult.

Interesting and informative is the Greek word translated as *sin* in the New Testament is *hamartia*, which means "to miss the mark" or "to err." In Greek tragedy *hamartia* refers to the protagonist's error or flaw that leads to a tragic reversal of fortune. The error or flaw can result from ignorance, erroneous judgment or bad character.

Socrates believed ignorance explains moral failures and maintained if people could appreciate the harm their sins do to themselves and others they would not "miss the mark." Aristotle understood sin as a failure to develop praiseworthy habits. He believed self-restraint and moderation in thoughts, actions, and feelings preclude sinful behavior. Noteworthy is temperance, a synonym for self-restraint, is one of the *four cardinal virtues* praised in the literature of both moral philosophy and theology. (The other three are fortitude, justice, and prudence.) C.S. Lewis characterized moral failures as misguided attempts to acquire a good thing in a bad way.

For example, sexual gratification is a good thing, but not by means of adultery; pain relief is a good thing, but not by means of drunkenness.

A striking example of ignorance, intemperance, and misguidance combining with tragic consequences is found in Edgar Allen Poe's short story, *The Black Cat*. Driven to unspeakable behavior by alcoholism, the story's protagonist and narrator gouges out the eye of his cat, an affectionate pet he had once loved. Eventually, he kills the cat by hanging it, offering a disturbing explanation for the despicable act:

> (I) hung it because I knew that it had loved me, and because I felt that it had given me no reason of offense; - hung because I knew that in so doing I was committing a sin - a deadly sin that would jeopardize my immortal soul as to place it - if such a thing were possible - even beyond the reach of the Most Merciful and Most Terrible God (Poe, 08/19/1843).

Fear of discovery, death or failure can also drive immoral conduct. In Woody Allen's comedy-drama, "Crimes and Misdemeanors," an adulterous doctor fears discovery of his philandering and resorts to murder as a cover up (1989). He is then burdened with guilt. Another drama, "Courage Under Fire," includes a soldier's dishonorable behavior in combat owing to his fear of death (1996). When the investigation of the incident is about to reveal his misdeed, he commits suicide. Fear of failure is so common that it is a type of phobia, *atychiphobia*. Atychiphobiacs make life more difficult by assiduously avoiding risk. In addition to the effort such avoidance requires, an exaggerated fear of risk limits life's possibilities.

Other People

In Jean-Paul Sartre's play, *No Exit*, the three main characters arrive in hell where their fate is to spend a sleepless eternity together in one small room. Each is well-suited to torment the other two occupants. At one point one of them says, "Hell is other people." Concerned that this line has been misunderstood, Sartre offers this clarification:

> ... "Hell is other people" has always been misunderstood. It has been thought that what I meant by that was that our relations with other people are always poisoned, that they are invariably hellish relations. But what I really mean is something totally different. I mean that if relations with someone else are twisted, vitiated, then that other person can only be hell. Why? Because ...when we think about ourselves, when we try to know ourselves, ...we use the knowledge of us which other people already have. We judge ourselves with the means other people have and have given us for judging ourselves. Into whatever I say about myself someone else's judgment always enters. Into whatever I feel within myself someone

else's judgment enters. ... But that does not at all mean that one cannot have relations with other people. It simply brings out the capital importance of all other people for each one of us (Woodward, 2010).

"Hell is other people," as Sartre intended, means if the only data we use for understanding ourselves is the opinions of others then, indeed, "Hell is other people." This is not to say we should be unconcerned with what others think of us. Rather, Sartre cautions against overreliance on the judgments of others in striving for self-understanding. Rudyard Kipling's classic poem, "If" expresses the balance Sartre would find agreeable: "If all men count with you, but none too much" (2018).

Comparing ourselves with other people is another inaccurate means for self-knowledge. The "Riddle of the Coal Miners" conveys the imprudence of looking to others for self-understanding.

Two men emerge from a coal mine after a long day of working. One has a face blackened with coal soot. The other's face is clean. They say goodbye to each other and return to their respective homes. The miner with the clean face washes his face before sitting down for dinner. The miner with the dirty face sits for dinner without washing. Question: Why does the miner with the clean face wash and the other, with the dirty face, not wash?

Answer: When they looked at each other after coming up from the mine each man assumed his face must look like the face of the other man.

Naive realism is an interesting psychological concept that explains much interpersonal conflict. It is the misguided belief that everyone will draw the same conclusion if they are working from the same set of facts. A story told by David Foster Wallace provides an example of naive realism.

There are two guys sitting in a bar in the remote Alaskan wilderness. One of the guys is religious, the other's an atheist, and they're arguing about the existence of God with that special intensity that comes after about the fourth beer. And the atheist says, "Look, it's not like I don't have actual reasons for not believing in God. It's not like I haven't ever experimented with the whole God-and-prayer thing. Just last month, I got caught away from the camp in a terrible blizzard, and I couldn't see anything, and I was totally lost, and it was fifty below, and so I did, I tried it: I fell to my knees in the snow and cried out, 'God, if there's a God, I'm lost in this blizzard, and I'm going to die if you don't help me!'"

And now, in the bar, the religious guy looks at the atheist all puzzled: "Well then, you must believe now," he says. "After all, here you are, alive."

The atheist rolls his eyes like the religious guy is a total simp: "No man, all that happened was that a couple of Eskimos just happen to come wandering by, and they showed me the way back to camp" (2009, pp. 17-23).

Difficulties with other people often result from naively believing if people agree on the facts they will agree on conclusions. This reasoning is specious because it fails to take into account the different personalities, experiences, and assumptions people bring to the analysis of any set of facts. Abandonment of naive realism is a sure way to make life less difficult.

Keeping bad company is yet another way other people make life excessively difficult. In *Renewing Your Spiritual Passion* Gordon MacDonald describes "very resourceful people" (VRP's) and "very draining people" (VDP's)(1997). The former provide encouragement and contribute to the growth of others in their relationships. Shakespeare's Polonius alludes to them with these words: "Those friends thou hast, and their adoption tried, grapple them unto thy soul with hoops of steel (*Hamlet*, 1.3). The latter receive far more than they give in their relationships. As suggested by their category ("very draining people"), they are demanding and exhausting. Anyone in a relationship with a VDP is in a toxic relationship. One book among many on such relationships is *Emotional Blackmail* by Susan Forward and Donna Frazier. Its subtitle provides a description of people to be avoided: *When the*

People in Your Life Use Fear, Obligation, and Guilt to Manipulate You (1998).

Regretting the Past

According to Oscar Wilde, "No man is rich enough to buy back his past" (2013, p. 132). All-consuming regret over past deeds and/or failures vitiates the present and darkens the future. Such regret can take the form of form of lamenting the life that might have been. In *Missing Out: In Praise of the Unlived Life,* psychiatrist Adam Phillips challenges the assumption that a hypothetical life would have been better than the life actually lived.

> Instead of feeling that we should have had a better life, he says, we should just live, as gratifyingly as possible, the life we have. Otherwise we are setting ourselves up for bitterness. What makes us think that we could have been a contender? Yet, in the dark of night, we do think this, and grieve that it wasn't possible. "And what was possible all too easily becomes the story of our lives," Phillips writes. "Our lived lives might become a protracted mourning for, or endless trauma about, the lives we were unable to live" (Acocella, 2013, p. 79).

Augusten Burroughs challenges the common wisdom that a dream should never be forsaken by asking, "If you spend 20 years chasing something, is it admirable to keep trying? Or did you pass admirable several miles back, and it's getting closer to straitjacket time?" (2016, p. 96). There are times when giving up the life we dreamed of is the only way to have the life waiting for us.

Bemoaning that Pleasure Is Transitory

The subject of pleasure has not lacked attention from eminent psychologists through the years. Freud spoke of the *will to pleasure* as a fundamental human drive. Murray included it (sentience) in his list of 27 psychogenic needs. And Paul Bloom devoted an entire book to analyzing and explaining it: *How Pleasure Works: The New Science of Why We Like What We Like* (2011). Considering our own thoughts and activities, would we expect to find anyone who would deny the importance of the pursuit of pleasure?

When the Buddha (Siddhartha Gautama) taught "suffering comes from desire" as one of the *Four Noble Truths* he meant the desire for a pleasurable experience not to end generates suffering. His prescription for averting this type of suffering is immersion in the present enjoyable experience without lamenting its impermanence. He understood anticipating the end of an enjoyable experience diminishes pleasure. Regretting that all good things come to an end is yet another way to make life more difficult.

IV. Is a Good Life Possible?

All lives are different, and some face hardships that others will never know. But we all share the same universe, the same laws of nature, and the same fundamental task of creating meaning and of mattering for ourselves and those around us in the brief amount of time we have in the world.

Three billion heartbeats. The clock is ticking.

\- Sean Carroll

The late Daniel Robinson opined, "The good life is active, contemplative, somewhat fatalistic, and selfless" (2004, p. 8). Few people are as qualified as Professor Robinson to speak about the characteristics of a good life. Widely recognized as a distinguished scholar in both psychology and philosophy, he believed a good life requires participation, reflection, acceptance, and charity. Each of these requirements is considered below.

The good life is active.

Novelist and poet Dorothy Sayers offers a scathing indictment of sloth, the antithesis of activity and one of the seven deadly sins:

It is the sin that believes in nothing, cares for nothing, seeks to know nothing, interferes with nothing, enjoys nothing, hates nothing, finds purpose in nothing, lives for nothing, and remains alive because there is nothing for which it will die (Fairlie, 1979, p. 114).

Speaking at the "Great March on Detroit" the Rev. Dr. Martin Luther King, Jr. asserted,

there are some things so dear, some things so precious, some things so eternally true, that they are worth dying for. And I submit to you that if a man has not discovered something that he will die for, he isn't fit to live (1963).

Likely there are many people who could not immediately identify something for which they would die. But this failure would not make them slothful. It is people who are indifferent to everything and have an interest in nothing who are disqualified for a good life.

Freud and Tolstoy believed work and love are integral to overall life contentment. Concerning work, Aristotle included it in his formula for happiness (*eudaimonia*). The psychological term *flow* is "total immersion in a task that is challenging yet closely matched with one's abilities" (Haidt, 2006, p. 95). In a state of flow people lose self-awareness and are nescient to the passing of time. The importance of meaningful activity for happiness is evident from a simple calculation: 35 years of employment (ages 21 to 55) consists of 70,000 hours at work (50 weeks per year times 40 hours per week). When experiencing boredom, time passes slowly. Conversely, the passing of time is imperceptible in a state of flow. The thought of spending 70,000 hours (approximately ten percent of an 80-year life) in a state of boredom underscores the influence of activity on a good life.

The good life is contemplative.

In the classic play *Inherit the Wind* one of the characters, Henry Drummond, emphasizes the one quality that elevates human beings above all other living things: "The ability to think! What other merit have we? The horse is stronger and swifter; the mosquito is more prolific; the butterfly is more beautiful; even the simple sponge is more durable" (Lawrence and Lee, 1955, 1.2). Aristotle believed since human beings have the unique faculty to engage in thought it constitutes the best possible life for them. He reasoned just as birds fly and fish swim because that is what they are made to do, so also human beings are acting compatibly with their nature when they are thinking. He also believed the pursuit of sensual pleasure is inferior to the pursuit of wisdom, which can be acquired only through contemplation. Since wisdom is necessary for the best possible life, contemplation is the superior activity. Socrates showed his agreement with Aristotle when he declared, "The unexamined life is not worth living" (Plato, 1966, 38a 5-6). This assertion, part of his self-defense at his trial for treason, expressed his belief that the best possible life includes reflection and introspection.

35

The good life is somewhat fatalistic.

It is important to note Professor Robinson proposes the good life is *somewhat fatalistic* rather than *fatalistic*. To be fatalistic is to believe life is a matter of living out an unalterable script written by a supernatural power from which any attempt at deviation is futile. At the other extreme is the resolve expressed by the political activist Angela Davis when she said, "I am no longer accepting the things I cannot change. I am changing the things I cannot accept" (2018). As with most extreme positions, fatalism and Davis' determination overreach. A more moderate view of life is offered by psychologist Martin Seligman in *What You Can Change ... and What You Can't* (1993). Like Robinson, Seligman believes some life conditions and personal attributes are subject to change and others are not. (Seligman does not include changing other people against their will in his list of changeable things.)

Stoicism is the philosophical counterpart to Seligman's psychological position. James Bond Stockdale put stoicism to the test as a POW in North Vietnam for nearly eight years. He credited his survival of isolation, starvation, and torture to Epictetus, a first century stoic philosopher. Stockdale said he retained his mental health by directing his thoughts and energy *only* to those things over which he had a measure of control. While he could not control whether he would be tortured, he could choose to resist as long as possible and what information he would provide. (He usually gave meaningless information.) He could not control whether he would be fed, but he could determine if he would eat his bowl of rice all at once or make it last as long as possible.

To deploy thoughts and actions toward things unchangeable guarantees frustration. To direct attention to things changeable contributes to serenity, as suggested by theologian Reinhold Niebuhr's prayer:

God, grant me the serenity to accept the things I cannot change,
Courage to change the things I can,
And wisdom to know the difference (2002, p. 735).

The good life is selfless.

Twenty-five centuries ago the Greek philosopher Heraclitus taught, "All things come into being by conflict of opposites" (2018). This is the case with attending to the needs of others. Theologian David Elton Trueblood offers a commendable view of altruism: "A man has made at least a start on discovering the meaning of human life when he plants shade trees under which he knows full well he will never sit (1951, p. 58).

In stark contrast is philosopher and novelist Ayn Rand's denigration of altruism:

If a man accepts the ethics of altruism, he suffers the following consequences (in proportion to the degree of his acceptance): (1) Lack of self-esteem – since his first concern in the realm of values is not how to live his life, but how to sacrifice it. (2) Lack of respect for others - since he regards mankind as a herd of doomed beggars crying for someone's help (1961, p. 49).

Aristotle's *Principle of the Golden Mean* teaches moral excellence is an intermediate position between the extremes of excess and deficiency. Applied to charity, Trueblood and Rand represent the extremes of altruism and egoism respectively. The former believes a good life is found in serving the interests of others without recompense, reward or recognition. The latter believes a good life is found in exclusive concern with one's own interests. Although Robinson uses the word "selfless" in characterizing a good life, he believes altruists benefit from their benevolence:

A great and exalting pleasure comes from enlarging the possibilities in the lives of others; this has to meet the fundamental objectives of the *hedonistic* individual. Indeed, there must be great joy and pleasure in the life of a Mother Teresa, a deep sense of satisfaction for a hero knowing that he or she has saved a life (2004, p. 8).

Moreover, his respect for Aristotle's approach to morality

compels the conclusion that Robinson intends "selfless" as the mean between the extremes of unadulterated altruism and unremitting egoism. He recognizes a completely selfless life is a theoretical construct rather than a life actually lived. Citing Arsitotle, Robinson writes:

> Aristotle recognizes the importance of a knowledge of what constitutes moral excellence, but he also knows the whole point of such knowledge is to permit one to act in accordance with such principles. Again, the *eudaimonic* life is one that is actually *lived* in a certain way, not one that is simply dissected philosophically and abstractly as some sort of hypothetical life (Robinson, 1989, p. 113).

The Greek mythological character Echo, as the result of a curse, lost her own voice and could speak only the last words spoken to her. Using her as a point-of-reference, psychologist Craig Malkin wrote of the healthy balance between self-interest and service to others that is necessary for a good life:

> At the heart of narcissism lies an ancient conundrum: how much should we love ourselves and how much should we love others? The Judaic sage and scholar Hillel the Elder summarized the dilemma this way: "If I am not for myself, who am I? And if I am only for myself, then what am I?" To remain healthy and happy, we all need a certain amount of investment in

ourselves. We need a voice, a presence of our own, to make an impact on the world and people around us or else, like Echo, we eventually become nothing at all (2015, pp. 13-14).

To a degree, but certainly not entirely, life is a solitary journey. Nietzsche addresses the difficulty and sometimes loneliness of this journey with these words:

No one can build you the bridge on which you, and only you, must cross the river of life. There may be countless trails and bridges and demigods who would gladly carry you across; but only at the price of pawning and forgoing yourself. There is one path in the world that none can walk but you. Where does it lead? Don't ask, walk! (2018).

References

Preface

Peck, M. (1978). *The road less traveled: A new psychology of love, traditional values and spiritual growth.* New York: Simon and Schuster.

Introduction

Frankl, V. (1959). *Man's search for meaning.* Boston, MA: Beacon Press.

Gehrig, L. (2018). Recovered from http://www.lougehrig.com/ on 08/16/2018.

Hemingway, E. (2014). *A farewell to arms.* Reprint edition. New York: Charles Scribner & Sons.

King, S. (2018). Recovered from https://www.goodreads.com quotes/1345766-life-sucks-then-you-die-on 08/09/2018.

Malikow, M. (2013). *The human predicament: Towards an understanding of the human condition.* Chipley, Florida. Theocentric Publishing Group.

I. What Is a Difficult Life?

Allport, G.W. & Oddbert, H.S. (1936). "Trait names: A psycho-lexical study." *Psychological Monograph: General and Applied*, 47, 171-220. (Whole No. 211).

Chesterton, G.K. (2001). *Heretics*. Charleston, SC: Create-Space Independent Publishing.

Durant, W. (1926). *The story of philosophy: The lives and opinions of the world's great philosophers from Plato to John Dewey*. New York: Pocket Books.

Egan, J. (2016). *3,000 astounding quotes*. Morrisville, NC: LuLu Publishing.

Frankl, V. (1959). *Man's search for meaning*. Boston, MA: Beacon Press.

Goleman, D. (1995). *Emotional intelligence: Why it can matter more than IQ*. New York: Bantam Books.

Jung, C. (1933). *Modern man in search of a soul*. (W.S. Dell and C.F. Baynes, translators). New York: Harcourt Brace Jovanovich Publishers.

Kierkegaard, S. (1980). *The Sickness unto death. A christian psychological exposition for upbuilding and awaken-*

ing. H. Hong and E. Hong (editors and translators). Princeton, NJ: Princeton University Press.

Peck, S. (1978). *The road less traveled: A new psychology of love, traditional values and spiritual growth.* New York: Simon and Schuster.

Pope, A. (2000). *Alexander Pope: Selected letters.* Howard Erskine-Hill (Editor). London: Oxford University Press.

Sapolsky, R. (2018). Recovered from https://www.roberts apolskyrocks.com/aggrssion-ii.html on 08/23/2018.

Smith, T. (2008). "Rowling's Harvard speech doesn't entrance all." National Public Radio: Morning Edition. June 6, 2008.

The Huffington Post. "Father 30 times over seeks break in child support." 05/18/20.

Yalom, I. (1989). *Love's executioner & other tales of psychotherapy.* New York: Basic Books.

II. Why Shouldn't Life Be Difficult?

Benatar, D. (2006). *Better never to have been: The harm of coming into existence.* Oxford, UK: Oxford University Press.

Camus, A. (1955). *The myth of Sisyphus and other essays.*New York: Alfred A. Knopf, Inc.

Dargay, C. (2018). Recovered from *https://www.quora.com on 09/07/2018.*

deBeauvoir, S. (2014). Recovered from Thinkexist.com on 07/07/2014.

Hobbes, T. (1994). *Leviathan.* Indianapolis, IN: Hackett Publishing Co., Inc.

James, W. (1902). *The varieties of religious experience: A study in human nature.* New York: The Modern Library. Random House.

Malikow, M. (2017). *Heroism as virtue: Reflecting on human greatness.* Chipley, FL: Theocentric Publishing.

Murray, H. (1938). *Explorations in personality.* New York: Oxford University Press.

Pope, A. (2018). "An essay on man." Recovered from https://www.poetryfoundation.org on 09/09/2018.

The unforgiven. (1992). David Webb Peoples, Writer. Clint
Eastwood, Director. Warner Pictures.

Wartenberg, T. (2008). *Existentialism*. Oxford,UK: One
World Publications.

Weber, B. (2016). "Hilary Putnam, giant of modern
philosophy dies, at 89." *New York Times*. 03/17/2016.

Yeats, W.B. (2014). Recovered from Thinkexist.com on
07/07/2014

III. How Life Is Made More Difficult than It Has to Be?

Apocella, J. (2013). "This is your life." *The New Yorker*.
02/25/2013.

Bloom, P. (2011). *How pleasure works: The new science of
why we like what we like*. New York: W.W. Norton
Company.

Burroughs, A. (2016). "Day tripping." *Psychology Today*.
September & October, 2016.

"Courage under fire." (1996). Twentieth Century Fox.

"Crimes and misdemeanors." (1989). Orion Pictures.

Forward, S. and Frazier, D. (1998). *Emotional blackmail: When the people in your life use fear, obligation, and guilt to manipulate you.* New York: HarperCollins Publishers.

Kipling, R. (2018). "If." Chicago, IL: The Poetry Foundation.

MacDonald, G. (1997). *Renewing your spiritual passion.* Nashville, TN: Thomas Nelson Publishers.

Nisen, M. & Groth, A. "27 psychological reasons why good people do bad things." *Business insider.* 8/27/2012.

Poe, E. (1843). "The black cat." *The Saturday evening post.* 08/19/1843.

Wallace, D. (2009). *This is water: Some thoughts, delivered on a significant occasion, about living a compassionate life.* New York: Little, Brown and Company.

Wilde, O. (2013). *The quotable Oscar Wilde: A collection of wit and wisdom.* Philadelphia, PA: The Running Press

Woodward, K. (2010). "The most famous thing Jean-Paul Sartre never said." Rick on Theatre. 06/09/2010.

IV. Is a Good Life Possible?

Davis, A. (2018). Recovered from https://www.goodreads. com /.../7767240-i-am-no-longer-accepting-the-things-i-cannot ...on 03/24/2018.

Fairlie, H. (1979). *The seven deadly sins today.* South Bend, IN: University of Notre Dame Press.

Haidt, J. (2006). *The happiness hypothesis: Finding modern truth in ancient wisdom.* New York: Perseus Books Group.

Heraclitus. (2018). Recovered from http:www.azquotes.com> Authors>Heraclitus on 03/10/2018.

King, M.L. (1963). "Great March on Detroit." Speech given 06/23/1963.

Lawrence, J. and Lee, R. (1955). *Inherit the wind.*

Malkin, C. (2015). *Rethinking narcissism. The secret to recognizing and coping with narcissists.* New York: HarperCollins Publishers.

Niebuhr, R. (2002). "The serenity prayer." *Bartlett's familiar quotations. (17th edition).* New York: Little, Brown and Company.

Max Malikow

Nietzsche, F. (2018). Recovered from https://www.goodreads. com/quotes/7625719-no-one-can-build-you-the-bridge-on-which--you-walk-on on 03/27/2018.

Plato (1966). *The apology*. Translated by H.N. Fowler. Cambridge, MA: Harvard University Press.

Rand, A. (1961). *The virtue of selfishness*. New York: Penguin Books.

Robinson, D. (1989). *Aristotle's psychology*. New York: Columbia University Press.

_____. (2004). *The great ideas of philosophy (2nd edition)*. Chantilly, VA: The Teaching Company.

Seligman, M. (1993). *What you can change ... and what you can't: The complete guide to self-improvement (learning to accept who you are)*. San Francisco, CA: Fawcett Columbine.

Trueblood, D. (1951). *The life we prize*. New York: Harper & Brothers Publishers.